Carving New Frontiers

Ron Benson

Lynn Bryan

Kim Newlove

Charolette Player

Liz Stenson

CONSULTANTS

Kathyrn D'Angelo

Susan Elliott-Johns

Diane Lomond

Ken MacInnis

Elizabeth Parchment

Prentice Hall Ginn Canada
Scarborough, Ontario

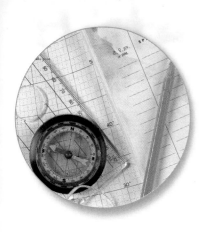

Contents

Pettranella   *picture book story by Betty Waterton*   4

A Pioneer Child's Day   *non-fiction narrative
by Bobbie Kalman and Tammy Everts*   14

More Than Anything Else   *picture book story
by Marie Bradby*   20

General Store   *poem by Rachel Field*   28

Dear Grandmother   *letter by Mickey Mitchell*   30
Pioneers   *list poem by Shannon Romeyn*

**How Two-Feather Was Saved from
Loneliness**   *legend by C. J. Taylor*   31

Fire Dragons and Flying Money
article by Sharon Stewart   36

The Inventor Thinks Up Helicopters
poem by Patricia Hubbell   40

 The Very Clever Device   *short story by Travis Forsyth*   42

 Ivory Soap   *report by Janaan Dibe*
Alexander Graham Bell   *profile by Angie Tse*   47

 Sojourner and Beyond   *article by Todd Mercer*   48

Hawaii, Here We Come!
diary by Sam Bendall   53

 Marisol and the Yellow Messenger
picture book story by Emilie Smith-Ayala   58

My Wish for Tomorrow   *art/commentaries*   66

 Born in Somalia   *personal narrative by Abdullahi Ugas*
Peace   *opinion by Sylvia Tang*   72

Bibliography

 Selections with this symbol are available on audio.

 This symbol indicates student writing.

Canadian selections are marked with this symbol.

Pettranella

by Betty Waterton
Illustrated by Ann Blades

Long ago in a country far away lived a little girl named Pettranella. She lived with her father and mother in the upstairs of her grandmother's tall, narrow house. Other houses just like it lined the street on both sides, and at the end of the street was the mill. All day and all night smoke rose from its great smokestacks and lay like a grey blanket over the city. It hid the sun and choked the trees, and it withered the flowers that tried to grow in the window boxes.

One dark winter night when the wind blew cold from the east, Pettranella's father came home with a letter. The family gathered around the table in the warm yellow circle of the lamp to read it. Even the grandmother came from her rooms downstairs to listen.

"It's from Uncle Gus in Canada," began her father. "He has his homestead there now, and is already clearing his land. Someday it will be a large farm growing many crops of grain." And then he read the letter aloud.

When he had finished, Pettranella said, "I wish we could go there, too, and live on a homestead."

Her parents looked at each other, their eyes twinkling with a secret. "We *are* going," said her mother. "We are sailing on the very next ship."

Pettranella could hardly believe her ears. Suddenly she thought of some things she had always wanted. "Can we have some chickens?" she asked. "And a swing?"

"You will be in charge of the chickens," laughed her father, "and I will put up a swing for you in our biggest tree."

"And Grandmother," cried Pettranella, "now you will have a real flower garden, not just a window box."

Pulling her close, the grandmother said gently, "But I cannot go to the new land with you, little one. I am too old to make such a long journey."

Pettranella's eyes filled with tears. "Then I won't go either," she said.

But in the end, of course, she did.

When they were ready to leave, her grandmother gave her a small muslin bag. Pettranella opened it and looked inside. "There are seeds in here!" she exclaimed.

"There is a garden in there," said the old lady. "Those are flower seeds to plant when you get to your new home."

"Oh, I will take such good care of them," promised Pettranella. "And I will plant them and make a beautiful garden for you."

So they left their homeland. It was sad, thought Pettranella, but it was exciting, too. Sad to say goodbye to everyone they knew, and exciting to be going across the ocean in a big ship.

But the winter storms were not over, and as the ship pitched about on the stormy seas everyone was seasick. For days Pettranella lay on her wooden bunk in the crowded hold, wishing she was back home in her clean, warm bed.

At last they reached the shores of Canada. Pettranella began to feel better. As they stood at the rail waiting to leave the ship, she asked, "Can we see our homestead yet?"

Not yet, they told her. There was still a long way to go.

Before they could continue their journey her father had to fill out many forms, and Pettranella spent hours and hours sitting on their round-topped trunk in a crowded building, waiting. So many people, she thought. Would there be room for them all?

Finally one day the last form was signed and they were free to go, and as they travelled up a wide river and across the lonely land, Pettranella knew that in this big country there would be room for everyone.

After many days they came to a settlement where two
rivers met and there they camped while the father got his
homestead papers. Then they bought some things they
would need: an axe and a saw, a hammer and nails, sacks of
food and seed, a plow and a cow and a strong brown ox, and
a cart with two large wooden wheels. And some chickens.

The ox was hitched to the cart, which was so full of all
their belongings that there was barely room for Pettranella
and her mother. Her father walked beside the ox, and the
cow followed.

The wooden wheels creaked over the bumpy ground, and
at first Pettranella thought it was fun, but soon she began
asking, "When are we going to get there?" and making rather
a nuisance of herself climbing in and out of the cart.

Often at night as they lay wrapped in their warm quilts beside the fire, they heard owls hooting, and sometimes wolves calling to one another; once they saw the northern lights.

One day as they followed the winding trail through groves of spruce and poplar, there was a sudden THUMP, CRACK, CRASH!

"What happened?" cried Pettranella, as she slid off the cart into the mud.

"We have broken a shaft," said her father. "One of the wheels went over a big rock."

"Now we'll never find our homestead!" wailed Pettranella, as they began to unload the cart. "We'll make a new shaft," said her father; and, taking his axe, he went into the woods to cut a pole the right size.

Pettranella helped her mother make lunch, then sat down on a log to wait. Taking the bag of seeds from her pocket, she poured them out into a little pile on her lap, thinking all the while of the garden she would soon be making.

Just then she heard something. A familiar creaking and squeaking, and it was getting closer. It had to be—it was— another ox cart!

"Somebody's coming!" she shouted, jumping up.

Her father came running out of the woods as the cart drew near. It was just like theirs, but the ox was black. The driver had a tanned, friendly face. When he saw their trouble, he swung down from his cart to help.

He helped the father make a new shaft, then they fastened it in place and loaded the cart again.

Afterwards they all had lunch, and Pettranella sat
listening while the grown-ups talked together. Their new
friend had a homestead near theirs, he said, and he invited
them to visit one day.

"Do you have any children?" asked Pettranella.

"A little girl just like you," he laughed, as he climbed into
his cart. He was on his way to get some supplies. Pettranella
waved goodbye as he drove off, and they set forth once again
to find their homestead. "Our neighbor says it isn't far now,"
said her father.

As they bumped along the trail, suddenly Pettranella
thought about the flower seeds. She felt in her pocket, but
there was nothing there. The muslin bag was gone!

"Oh, oh! Stop!" she cried. "The seeds are gone!"

Her father halted the ox. "I saw you looking at them before lunch," said her mother. "You must have spilled them there. You'll never find them now."

"I'm going back to look anyway," said Pettranella, and, before they could stop her, she was running back down the trail.

She found the log, but she didn't find any seeds. Just the empty muslin bag.

As she trudged back to the cart, her tears began to fall. "I was going to make such a beautiful garden, and now I broke my promise to Grandmother!"

"Maybe you can make a vegetable garden instead," suggested her mother, but Pettranella knew it wouldn't be the same. "I don't think turnips and cabbages are very pretty," she sighed.

It was later that afternoon, near teatime, when they found their homestead.

Their own land, as far as they could see! Pettranella was so excited that for a while she forgot all about her lost seeds.

That night they slept on beds of spruce and tamarack boughs cut from their own trees. What a good smell, thought Pettranella, snuggling under her quilt.

The next morning her father began to put up a small cabin; later he would build a larger one. Then he started to break the land. A small piece of ground was set aside for vegetables, and after it was dug, it was Pettranella's job to rake the earth and gather the stones into a pile.

"Can we plant the seeds now?" she asked when they had finished.

"Not yet," said her mother, "it's still too cold."

One morning they were awakened by a great noise that filled the sky above them. "Wild geese!" shouted the father, as they rushed outside to look. "They're on their way north. It's really spring!"

Soon squirrels chattered and red-winged blackbirds sang, a wobbly-legged calf was born to the cow, and sixteen baby chicks hatched.

"Now we can plant the garden," said the mother, and they did.

Early the next morning Pettranella ran outside to see if anything had sprouted yet. The soil was bare; but a few days later when she looked, she saw rows of tiny green shoots.

If only I hadn't lost Grandmother's seeds, she thought, flowers would be coming up now, too.

One warm Sunday a few weeks later, Pettranella put on a clean pinafore and her best sunbonnet and went to help her father hitch up the ox, for this was the day they were going to visit their neighbors.

As the ox cart bumped and bounced down the trail over which they had come so many weeks before, Pettranella thought about the little girl they were going to visit. She will probably be my very best friend, she thought to herself.

Suddenly her father stopped the cart and jumped down. "There's the rock where we broke the shaft," he said. "This time I will lead the ox around it."

"There's where we had lunch that day," said her mother.

"And there's the log I was sitting on when I lost the seeds," said Pettranella. "And look! LOOK AT ALL THOSE FLOWERS!"

There they were. Blowing gently in the breeze, their bright faces turned to the sun and their roots firm in the

Canadian soil—Grandmother's flowers.

"Oh! Oh!" cried Pettranella, "I have never seen such beautiful flowers!"

Her mother's eyes were shining as she looked at them. "Just like the ones that grew in the countryside back home!" she exclaimed.

"You can plant them beside our house," said her father, "and make a flower garden there."

Pettranella did, and she tended it carefully, and so her promise to her grandmother was not broken after all.

But she left some to grow beside the trail, that other settlers might see them and not feel lonely; and to this very day, Pettranella's flowers bloom each year beside a country road in Manitoba.

ABOUT THE AUTHOR   BETTY WATERTON

As a child, Betty Waterton "loved to read . . . write poetry and draw." She often sent poems to the local paper, and even had a poem published in the *Vancouver Sun*, for which she was paid one dollar. She wrote her first book, *A Salmon for Simon*, when her grandson lived on a small island. Since then she has published over ten books. Betty now lives in Sidney, British Columbia.

A Pioneer Child's Day

by Bobbie Kalman and Tammy Everts

"Goodness, John, wake up. It's five o'clock already!" Mother called upstairs. John opened his eyes. Through the small window in his bedroom he could see that the sky was still dark. John stretched quickly and jumped out of bed—the morning chores had to be done.

When his feet hit the warm floor, he was thankful it wasn't winter. In winter he had to hop from foot to foot to keep his toes from freezing. The water in his washbowl would be so cold that a thin layer of ice floated on the top! After dressing in his cotton shirt and comfortable trousers, John hurried downstairs and rushed out to the barn to join his father.

Morning chores

Together, Father and John milked the cows, cleaned the calf pens, and fed the livestock. After giving his pet calf a quick pat, John returned to the house for breakfast.

John takes a moment to pet his cow, Daisy. Daisy wonders if John has a tasty treat hidden in his hand.

A hearty breakfast

In the kitchen, Mother and sister Emily bustled around the fireplace preparing breakfast. Soon Father came in, and the family sat down to a hearty breakfast of sizzling bacon, fried potatoes, hot buckwheat pancakes with sweet maple syrup, fresh bread and preserves, and donuts.

Time for school

John and Emily took the lunch box that their mother had prepared for them and walked the half-hour trek to school. There was a spelling bee that day, and Emily's team won, as usual. No one could spell as well as Emily. John was happy when the day was over because he hated to see Emily gloat!

More chores

After school, John enjoyed helping Father care for the animals. He spread fresh hay in the stalls of the cows, oxen, calves, pigs, and sheep so the animals could have soft, clean beds. He fed the animals and milked the cows. Finally, it was time for dinner.

Settler children did adult work such as caring for the oxen.

Time for dinner

It was finally dinnertime! The kitchen was warm and smelled good. John's stomach growled hungrily as Father said a prayer of thanks and served dinner. Emily and John received their servings last because, in those days, adults were always served first.

Finally, Father placed a heaping plate of food in front of each child. The plates were piled high with smoked ham, potato cakes, baked beans, butternut squash, johnny cake, and pickled

At the end of a long day's work, the family enjoys sitting down to a hearty dinner. Everyone is very hungry!

beets. John's face lit up when he saw that Mother had prepared his favorite dish—fried apples 'n' onions!

Emily was not as happy to see the apples 'n' onions, which she didn't like at all. She did not complain, however. She was supposed to eat everything on her plate without arguing. The children ate quickly as they listened to their parents talk. Emily and John were not allowed to speak unless they were spoken to, but that didn't matter. Their hard work had made them too hungry to talk!

Happy evenings by the fire

After dinner, Mother and Emily washed the dishes and cleaned the kitchen. Father sat by the fireplace and whittled a new handle for his axe. John played with some building blocks his father had made for him.

Evenings were a happy time when the family sat together around the fire and ate apples, beechnuts, and popcorn. At nine o'clock, everyone went to bed. They needed plenty of rest for the next busy day.

It is Emily's job to make butter. Churning the thick cream into soft butter is a hard job that takes hours, but someone has to do it! The fresh, delicious result is worth the effort.

Thirsty cows and horses need water to drink. John uses a yoke to carry water from the well to the barn. The yoke is worn across his neck and shoulders. It helps John carry loads that would be too heavy otherwise.

A full, busy life

Early settler children had lives that were very different from those of boys and girls today. Difficult work was a part of every day. In order to have enough food and clothing, the entire family had to work hard. Boys and girls began to do chores as soon as they were able to walk and talk. Parents loved their children, but they were very strict. They had to be—a family needed co-operation and teamwork to get everything done.

Emily helps her mother spin thread, weave cloth, make candles, and sew clothing. In those days girls learned how to sew when they were young. By the time she was four years old, Emily had already stitched her first quilt square!

John and Emily "horse around" on the family wagon. Giddyup!

Using their imagination

Even though boys and girls worked hard, they always found time for fun. Many children today have a huge variety of toys, games, and activities from which to choose. Settler children had to amuse themselves with simple games and a few homemade toys. Most of these games were played outdoors, using objects found around the farm or in the community. An old barrel hoop provided hours of fun when it was rolled with a stick. With a bit of pretending, a fence could be a bucking horse to ride. A sturdy board laid over a tree stump became a simple seesaw. Rocks, leaves, and branches created imaginary houses and forts. A child's only limit was his or her imagination.

Not every minute was devoted to work. Children played with simple but fun toys.

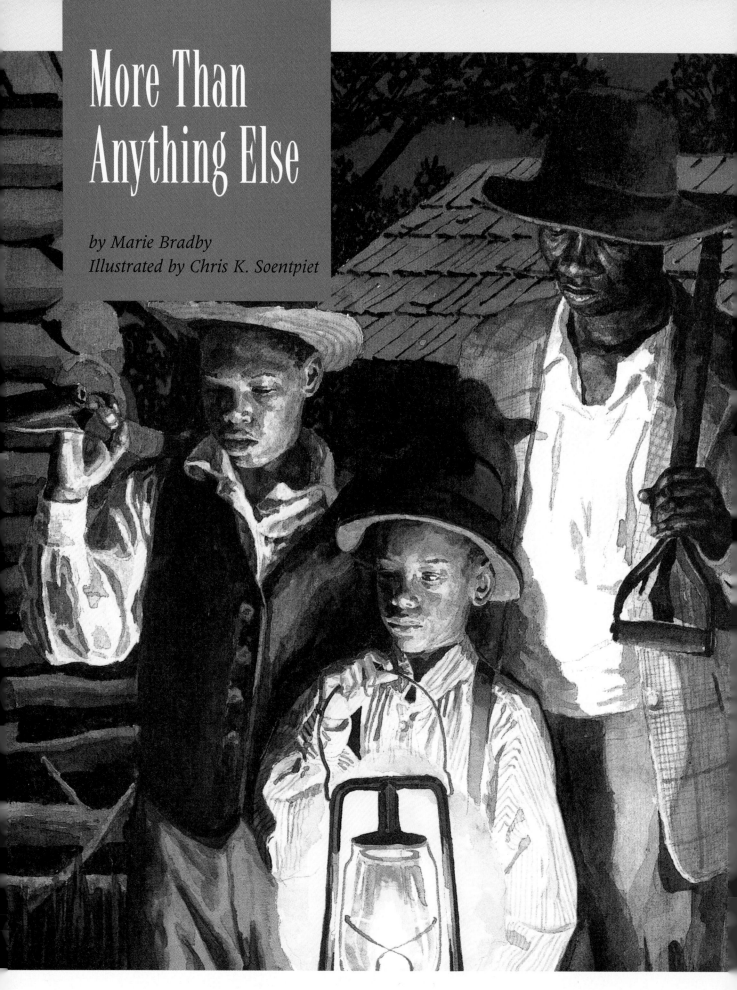

More Than Anything Else

by Marie Bradby
Illustrated by Chris K. Soentpiet

Before light—while the stars still twinkle—Papa, my brother John, and I leave our cabin and take the main road out of town, headed to work.

The road hugs the ridge between the Kanawha River and the mountain. We travel it by lantern. My stomach rumbles, for we had no morning meal. But it isn't really a meal I want, though I would not turn one down.

More than anything else, I want to learn to read.

But for now, I must work. From sunup to sundown, we pack salt in barrels at the saltworks.

A white mountain of salt rises above Papa's head. All day long we shovel it, but it refuses to grow smaller.

We stop only to grab a bite—sweet potatoes and
corn cakes that Papa has brought along in his coat
pocket. As I eat every crumb of my meal, I stare at the
white mountain. Salt is heavy and rough. The shiny
white crystals leave cuts on your hands, your arms,
your legs, the soles of your feet.

My arms ache from lifting the shovel, but I do not
think about the pain there. I think about the hunger
still in my head—reading. I have seen some people—
young and old—do it. I am nine years old and I
know, if I had a chance, I could do it, too.

I think there is a secret in those books.

In the chill of the evening, I follow Papa and John
back up the road, stopping to catch a frog. The frog
wiggles and slips, but I hold on tight and let go when
I want to.

There is something different about this place where we live now. All people are free to go where they want and do what they can. Book learning swims freely around in my head and I hold it long as I want.

Back in town, coal miners, river men, loggers, and coopers gather on the corner. They are worn-out as me, but full of tales.

I see a man reading a newspaper aloud and all doubt falls away. I have found hope, and it is as brown as me.

I see myself the man. And as I watch his eyes move across the paper, it is as if *I* know what the black marks mean, as if *I* am reading. As if everyone is listening to *me*. And I hold that thought in my hands.

I will work until I am the best reader in the county. Children will crowd around me, and I will teach *them* to read.

But Papa taps me on the shoulder. "Come on." And John tugs at my shirt. They don't see what I see. They don't see what I can be.

We hurry home. "Mama, I have to learn to read," I say. She holds my hand and feels my hunger racing fast as my heart.

It is a small book—a blue the color of midnight. She gives it to me one evening in the corner of our cabin, pulling it from under the clothes that she washes and irons to make a little money.

She doesn't say where she got it. She can't read it herself. But she knows this is something called the alphabet. She thinks it is a sing-y kind of thing. A song on paper.

After work, even though my shoulders still ache and my legs are stained with salt, I study my book. I stare at the marks and try to imagine their song.

I draw the marks on the dirt floor and try to figure out what sounds they make, what story their picture tells.

But sometimes I feel I am trying to jump without legs. And my thoughts get slippery, and I can't keep up with what I want to be, and how good I will feel when I learn this magic, and how people will look up to me.

I can't catch the tune of what I see. I get a salt-shovelling pain and feel my dreams are slipping away.

I have got to find him—that newspaper man.

25

I look everywhere.
Finally, I find that brown face of hope.
He tells me the song—the sounds the marks make.
I jump up and down singing it. I shout and laugh like when I was baptized in the creek. I have jumped into another world and I am saved.

But I have to know more. "Tell me more," I say.
"What's your name?" he asks.
"Booker," I say.
And he takes the sound of my name and draws it
on the ground.

I linger over that picture. I know I can hold it
forever.

ABOUT THE AUTHOR   MARIE BRADBY

Marie Bradby was born in Alexandria, Virginia. She began
her career as a full-time journalist, writing for publications such
as *National Geographic*. She then went on to become a mother and
fiction writer. *More Than Anything Else* has received several awards and
honors. Marie now lives with her family in Louisville, Kentucky.

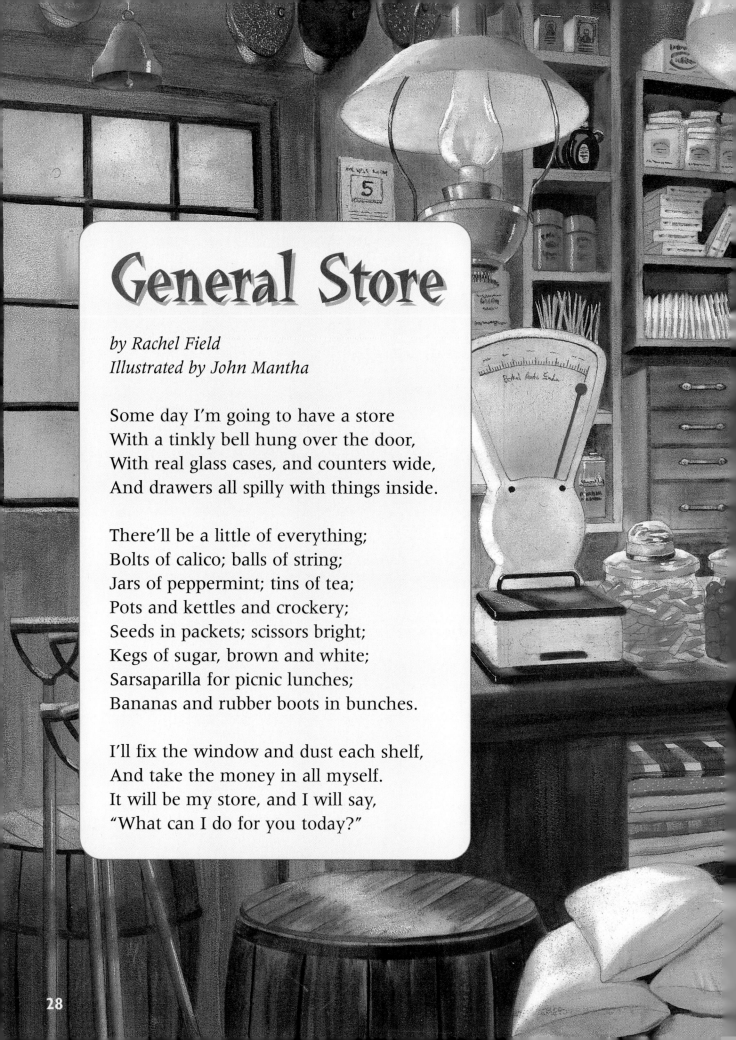

General Store

by Rachel Field
Illustrated by John Mantha

Some day I'm going to have a store
With a tinkly bell hung over the door,
With real glass cases, and counters wide,
And drawers all spilly with things inside.

There'll be a little of everything;
Bolts of calico; balls of string;
Jars of peppermint; tins of tea;
Pots and kettles and crockery;
Seeds in packets; scissors bright;
Kegs of sugar, brown and white;
Sarsaparilla for picnic lunches;
Bananas and rubber boots in bunches.

I'll fix the window and dust each shelf,
And take the money in all myself.
It will be my store, and I will say,
"What can I do for you today?"

Dear Grandmother

Dear Grandmother,

Life is different now that I live in a covered wagon. We have to go fishing for our own fish. We have to go hunting for our own deer, and we have to pick berries for dessert. The two oxen are slow but some day we will reach the West. I have seen trout, foxes, blue jays, robins, and rabbits. I wonder if we will ever get off this wagon. I am starting to miss my family folks back East.

Love,
Simon

Mickey Mitchell
Age 9

I chose to write about a covered wagon because I sometimes wish that I was a pioneer. They had risky and challenging choices to make.

Mickey Mitchell

Pioneers

Pioneers
Wanderers, Travellers
Adventuring, Exploring, Discovering
Taking risks
Bold Settlers

Shannon Romeyn
Age 9

I wrote this because I am very interested in pioneers. I like pioneers because they are very adventurous.

Shannon Romeyn

How Two-Feather Was Saved from Loneliness

Written and illustrated by C. J. Taylor

ong ago the Earth was a cold and lonely place. No one knew how to make fire. There were very few people and they wandered far in search of food.

Two-Feather was lonely and hungry. All winter long he had met no one. All he had to eat was the bark he cut off the trees and the roots he dug out from under the snow.

He was glad when at last spring came. The sun grew warmer and the ice melted from the lakes and rivers. As he knelt to drink from a rushing stream, he caught sight of his face in the water and he felt lonely again: "How I wish," he thought, "I could see another face."

To forget his loneliness, Two-Feather lay down to sleep on the soft moss. He was awakened by a voice calling his name. He was afraid to open his eyes and find it was only a dream. But the voice came again and the rustle of leaves told him someone was near.

He opened his eyes and was frightened to find a strange figure above him. His fear passed as he saw a woman, lovely as spring, with long soft hair. He held out his arms to her, but she moved away.

He tried again and again to touch her, but always she stayed just beyond his reach. All day he followed her.

At nightfall they came to a lake. He could not get close to her, so he made a drum and, in the moonlight, sang of his love.

"Please," he begged. "I am so lonely and you are so lovely. Stay with me and I will love you and look after you forever."

"I have come to look after you, Two-Feather," she said softly. "If you do what I say, you will never be lonely again."

"What would you have me do?" he asked.

"Follow me," she said, and turned away.

He followed her over mountains, through forests, across streams, always afraid she would get away from him. If he tried to catch up with her, she hurried on ahead. But when he grew tired or hungry and slowed down to rest or eat, she waited for him. After many days, they came to a vast meadow.

At last she stopped and rose up into the air, hovering over him like a bird.

"Two-Feather," she said, "gather some dry grass into a little pile, then take two sticks and rub them together."

Soon sparks flew. The little pile of grass caught fire. Then the tall grass and soon the whole meadow was ablaze. Two-Feather had never seen fire before and he was frightened. Would it spread forever and destroy the Earth?

But the soft voice reassured him. "It will be all right, Two-Feather," she said.

When all the grass in the meadow had burned and the fire died down, she spoke again.

"Now, take hold of my hair and pull me over the burned ground."

"I cannot do that," Two-Feather protested. "I cannot hurt you for I love you."

"If you love me, Two-Feather, you must trust me and do as I say," she said gently.

Two-Feather did as she asked. He pulled her back and forth over the burned meadow. Her hair in his hand was softer than anything he had ever felt before. She seemed to grow lighter and lighter as he pulled.

When he finished and turned, she was no longer there. But where he had pulled her, green shoots appeared. It was the first corn ever grown.

As the corn grew tall and ripened, people found their way to it. Now they no longer had to wander in search of food. They built houses and a village.

Two-Feather married and had children. He was no longer lonely but he never forgot the Corn Goddess. Each summer as he held the first ears of corn, he felt in his hands again the softness of her hair.

ABOUT THE AUTHOR C. J. TAYLOR

C. J. Taylor was born in Montreal and raised in the Eastern Townships, Quebec. Her mother was of German and British descent and her father was a Mohawk. She first started painting when she was sixteen years old. Her work is about the traditional lifestyles of North American Aboriginal Peoples, and how they live in harmony with nature.

Fire Dragons and Flying Money

Amazing Chinese Inventions

Hop on your bicycle, grab your umbrella, or jot a note on a piece of paper. You can't do any of these things without using a Chinese invention!

by Sharon Stewart

Everybody knows that scientists have made a lot of inventions and discoveries. Not many people know, though, that many of these important discoveries were first made in China.

Dazzling Discoveries

Have you ever wondered why cups and saucers and plates are called "china"? It's because long ago the Chinese invented a special kind of pottery called *porcelain*. Porcelain dishes were so thin and delicate that you could see a shadow through them. Traders brought these wonderful dishes from China to Europe, so people there called them "china."

Porcelain plate

Silk cloth was invented in China. First, the cocoons of silkworms were soaked in hot water. Then the long shining threads were unwound, and woven into gleaming cloth.

Making paper. *The paper pulp is left behind on the screen.*

Paper was first made in China more than two thousand years ago. What was it made out of? All kinds of things—the bark from mulberry trees, a plant called hemp, and even old fishing nets. These materials were boiled with water to make a soft gooey paste called *pulp*. Then the pulp and water were strained through flat screened boxes. Later, the paper sheets were peeled off the screens and hung up to finish drying.

Paper money and printing block

More Incredible Inventions

The compass was another important Chinese invention. Chinese scientists learned that a kind of rock called *lodestone* did a very strange thing. If a small bar of it was hung from a string, it would always turn until it pointed north and south. Then someone fastened a bar of lodestone to a bit of wood and floated it in water. It did the same thing. So did a steel needle that had been rubbed with a piece of lodestone. The Chinese had found a way to tell direction, no matter where they were on land or sea.

The Chinese used paper in all sorts of ways. They invented wallpaper, and also made clothing and even armor out of paper. They also invented the process of printing words on paper using *type*—little blocks of wood or metal with symbols carved on them. The blocks were brushed with ink, then pressed on rolls or sheets of paper. The Chinese also invented the world's first printed paper money. This new kind of money was so light that a breeze could blow it away. So the Chinese called it "flying money."

Floating compass

Flying dragon rocket

If you want to find more Chinese inventions, just look around you. Matches, umbrellas, and wheelbarrows were all invented in China. So was the *chain drive*—that's the same kind of chain that turns the wheels on your bicycle. That's not the end of the list of Chinese inventions, either.

The Chinese also invented gunpowder, and from that came many more inventions—fireworks, guns, and rockets. Chinese armies and navies used a special kind of war rocket called a "flying dragon." It had two rockets at each end, and a flock of rocket arrows inside it.

Chinese wheelbarrow *with sail. The sail made it easier to carry the load.*

Kites *were invented in China long ago. People flew them for fun, but fishers also used them to carry fishing lines.*

Some people believe that just three great inventions have had the most effect on the way we live today. They are the compass, gunpowder, and paper and printing. As you've just found out, every single one of them is Chinese!

The Inventor Thinks Up Helicopters

by Patricia Hubbell
Illustrated by Marc Mongeau

"Why not
a
vertical
whirling
winding
bug,
that hops like a cricket
crossing a rug,
that swerves like a dragonfly
testing his steering,
twisting and veering?
Fleet as a beetle.
Up
down
left
right,
jounce, bounce, day and night.
It could land in a pasture the size of a dot . . .
Why not?"

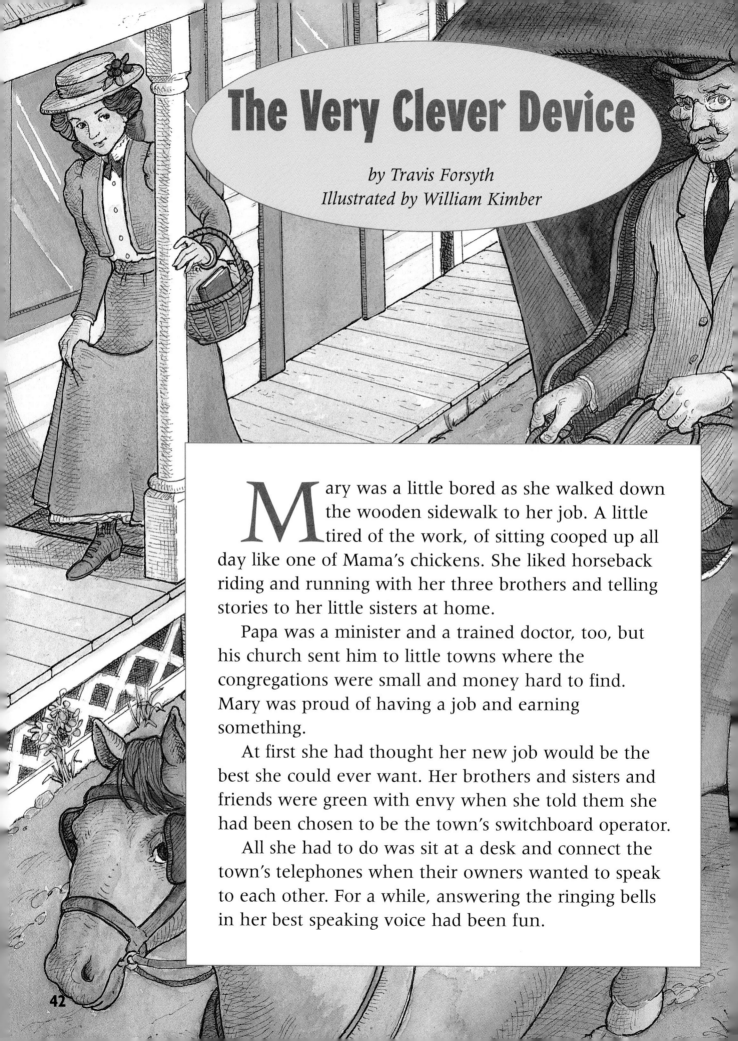

The Very Clever Device

by Travis Forsyth
Illustrated by William Kimber

Mary was a little bored as she walked down the wooden sidewalk to her job. A little tired of the work, of sitting cooped up all day like one of Mama's chickens. She liked horseback riding and running with her three brothers and telling stories to her little sisters at home.

Papa was a minister and a trained doctor, too, but his church sent him to little towns where the congregations were small and money hard to find. Mary was proud of having a job and earning something.

At first she had thought her new job would be the best she could ever want. Her brothers and sisters and friends were green with envy when she told them she had been chosen to be the town's switchboard operator.

All she had to do was sit at a desk and connect the town's telephones when their owners wanted to speak to each other. For a while, answering the ringing bells in her best speaking voice had been fun.

But there were only five telephones in town so far, and Mary didn't have much to do. It was getting to be summer, and the little switchboard room was stifling hot.

Mary yawned. The switchboard was quiet, only Mrs. Cullins was giving her list to the grocer. Mary opened up her O. Hinty adventure story and started to read. The heroine was on a ship going around the Cape of Good Hope in stormy winter weather, but all Mary could think of was saddling up Honeycut.

A bell rang on her board. With a start, she looked up and saw it was the bell connecting her with the next town.

"Hello, Telephone Company," she said in her most beautifully polite telephone voice.

"Mary, is that you?" It was her friend Iris, who was the switchboard girl in the next town.

"Oh, it's so hot," Mary started to complain.

"I know, but never mind! You can't guess! An *automobile* is coming through our town, and it will go right on to yours after!"

"What?!" Mary shrieked. Her father and brothers had been talking about automobiles for the last few months, so she knew what they were. A neat new invention, her papa had said, using some kind of engine to drive a little cart over the road with nothing pulling it. No horses of any kind.

"When? Do you know what time?" Mary asked, very excited.

"About noon. It should be through your town around noon," Iris said. "Got to go, Mrs. Cabots is ringing."

Iris rang off, and Mary immediately began making phone calls. This was important. She had to warn the whole town.

By noon everyone who could walk lined the streets. There were little kids—one of them her grimy little sister. Mary had found one of her brothers in the general store and told him to go home and tell Mama and Papa, so her family wouldn't miss out on the sight. Shopkeepers had closed their businesses to watch the thing go by.

The whole town was watching the twisty, red clay road when the automobile appeared as a tiny black bump on the horizon. Covered with thick dirt and clay, it chugged slowly up the road on its wire wheels to where everyone was waiting.

Two men sat in the front seat and two women in the back. The townspeople stood quietly on the sidewalk, staring with their mouths open, as the people in the car drove slowly down the main street, pretending not to notice the crowd.

The women in the back seat looked neither to the right nor to the left, but held on to their big picture hats with both hands, their faces hidden behind thick veils that were supposed to keep out the dirt.

"But I wouldn't want to *own* one," her brother Travis said later at dinner.

"No, there's nothing as beautiful as a good horse," Papa agreed. "The automobile is a very clever device. It took a lot of doing to think of such a thing, and then actually make it. We don't need to hurt Mr. Ford's feelings by telling him that we'll always prefer the horse."

"And you did well to tell everyone, Mary," said Mama. "I don't imagine an automobile will ever be seen around here again."

AUTHOR   TRAVIS FORSYTH

Travis Forsyth was born in Pittsburgh, Pennsylvania. She spent many summers in St. Petersburg, Florida, with her grandparents. Every night they told old stories that seemed "far more real than anything that had happened that day. 'The Very Clever Device' is one of those stories."

Ivory Soap

Ivory soap was invented in 1879. The company who invented it was Proctor and Gamble. The soap shape is a rectangle and it floats. Ivory soap was invented by accident in a factory. It was invented by a worker. The worker forgot to turn off the soap machine and too much air got into the soap. That is why it floats.

Janaan Dibe
Grade 3

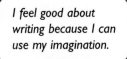

I feel good about writing because I can use my imagination.

Janaan Dibe

Alexander Graham Bell

Alexander Graham Bell will always be remembered as the father of the electric telephone. Bell was one of the many people working to make an instrument for speech communications. In 1874 and 1875 he began to work on his invention. He did experiments with devices to help people who could not hear.

On March 10th 1876, Bell sent the first sentence over the telephone. The first words he spoke to his assistant, Thomas Watson, were "Mr. Watson, come here. I want you."

Angie Tse
Grade 3

I love reading and writing so I loved doing the research for this profile.

Angie Tse

Sojourner and Beyond

by Todd Mercer
Illustrated by Dave McKay

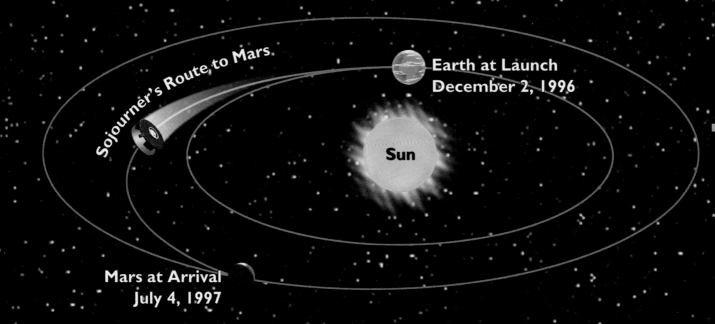

Sojourner's Route to Mars

**Earth at Launch
December 2, 1996**

Sun

**Mars at Arrival
July 4, 1997**

Journey across space. The Pathfinder spacecraft carries Sojourner to Mars.

In the past, explorers went on long journeys to new frontiers. They mapped the way to places where pioneers later settled. Today, the frontier is in space, and the explorers are robots travelling in spacecraft. Their mission is to explore new worlds where humans may live one day.

From Earth to Mars

The most exciting space frontier today is on the planet Mars. Why Mars? The answer is that it's the closest planet to Earth. It's also the planet that's most like Earth. One scientist says, "Mars is the only other planet that people would be able to live on in the next hundred years. We need to understand it to be able to send people there safely."

On Dec. 2, 1996, the Pathfinder spacecraft was launched from Earth. On July 4, 1997, it landed on Mars, and what an incredible landing it was! After the spacecraft entered Mars' atmosphere, air bags on it inflated like balloons. These airbags cushioned the spacecraft's hard landing.

When Pathfinder hit the planet, it bounced a number of times before coming to rest. Slowly the balloons emptied. Then the sides of the spacecraft opened like a flower.

A Robot Inside!

The most exciting part of the mission was still ahead, though. Inside Pathfinder was a very special cargo—a six-wheeled, 65-cm long robot rover called Sojourner. Sojourner was powered by the sun. It could move around Mars' rough surface at speeds of about 40 cm per minute.

Some of Sojourner's movements were directed by a computer scientist back on Earth. It was almost like operating a remote control toy car. Of course, the big difference was that this robot "car" was 191 million kilometres away!

◀ **Climbing over rocks.** *Scientists watch a copy of Sojourner perform.*

Sojourner on Mars. ▶
The rover is still aboard the spacecraft.

Yogi

Sojourner at work. *The rover checks a rock that scientists named Yogi.*

Sojourner could also make simple decisions on its own. It had lasers that told it when objects like rocks were in its path. Then its computer brain could decide to go around them.

The rover carried out its mission as planned. It collected color pictures and information about Mars for 30 Martian days, or *sols* (24.6 hours). Maybe some day in the very distant future, people will look back on the little robot's discoveries and call it one of Mars' first pioneers.

Did You Know?

The Sojourner received its name from Valerie Ambroise who won an essay-writing contest. She suggested the remote rover should be named after Sojourner Truth, an African-American who promoted rights for all people. "Sojourner" also means traveller.

Finding Out More About Mars

Scientists plan to send spacecraft to Mars every two years until about 2004. Some of the craft will contain robot rovers like Sojourner. However, these robots will be able to move faster and farther than Sojourner. Scientists hope they will tell us even more about Mars. Then, in about 2005, another robot mission will bring back soil and rock samples from Mars. This will help experts determine if there ever was life on Mars.

Some years after these last robot explorers, a mission will go to Mars with astronauts aboard. Maybe you or one of your friends will be among them!

Sojourner's big brother. *"Rocky 7" is now being tested in the Mojave Desert. The surface conditions there are like those on Mars.*

Fabulous Mars Facts

- **Mars is the fourth planet away from the sun and the closest to Earth.**
- **Mars, like Earth, has seasons.**
- **Temperatures where the Sojourner travelled were -26°C by day and -87°C by night.**
- **Scientists have found evidence that some form of life may have existed on Mars more than 3.6 million years ago.**
- **A volcano on Mars called Olympus Mons is 3 times the height of Mt. Everest, the highest mountain on Earth.**

Explore Mars for Yourself

You might want to explore Mars for yourself on these web sites.
- **www.jpl.nasa.gov/mars**
- **www.mgcm.arc.nasa.gov**

Hawaii, Here We Come!

by Sam Bendall

One day, Sam's parents tell him and his brother Charlie that the family is going to move. Not to a new house, though. They're going to live on a forty-foot sailboat (about 12 m). Next stop, Hawaii!

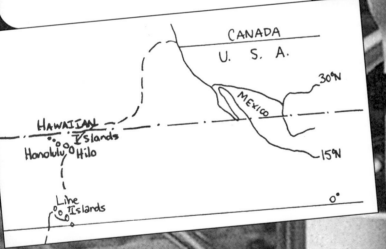

May 24

Dear Diary,

My friend Tristan gave me this diary yesterday when they had a going away party for me at Glenlyon School. I was only there one year, but I sure made a lot of good friends, and I know I'm going to miss them. The whole class came down to the boat to say goodbye, and after each classmate took a guided tour through *Kluane II*, we toasted to the trip with ice-cream cones. Since *Kluane* doesn't have a freezer, that ice-cream cone will be my last one for a while.

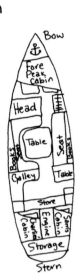

May 25

Dear Diary,

I can't tell you how awful this last 24 hours has been. Everyone is seasick except Mom. We are all really miserable because *Kluane* is knocking about all over the place so we can barely stand up. I have to hold on to the boat all the time—even when I'm sleeping. They gave me seasick medicine, which helps a bit, but it makes me really tired.

May 27

Dear Diary,

Sick today.

May 29

Dear Diary,

I'm writing to you now because I may not get another chance for a while. Dark clouds like I've never seen before are coming in fast. I know Dad is worried because all the sails have been reefed—that means made smaller. He keeps listening to our Sony shortwave radio for weather reports.

June 6

Dear Diary,

I know it has been a long time since I wrote to you, but I couldn't see for almost a week. That's because I touched a medicine patch I was wearing and got some of the medicine in my eyes. Boy, I hope I never go through that again! Luckily the problem only lasted a week, and it wasn't permanent. So, now I'll try to remember all the things that have happened lately.

The best news is that Charlie now has a friend. He was getting very lonely before and driving me crazy. Now we have a pet albatross following us. Charlie has named him "Albert Trossie." He does wonderful tricks in flight, especially for food, so we throw him all our edible garbage.

Charlie and I looked up "albatross" in our bird book. We discovered that these birds can live a long time at sea and are well known to oceangoing vessels. Albatrosses need strong air currents to fly and have incredibly long wings. They have been found as far away as 3200 kilometres from their babies—that's as far away as the distance between Whitehorse and Vancouver!

The book also says that they nest on land in shallow grooves of mud or soil. Both the males and females incubate and feed their young. Albatrosses convert food that they eat into an oily substance in their stomachs so that it can be stored without deterioration for long periods of time. Yuck! When albatrosses choose their mates, they do a spectacular courtship dance in flight and stay with that mate for life.

So I guess that's why Charlie spends his entire day on deck with Albert Trossie. Albert's chosen Charlie!

June 7
Dear Diary,
   The weather has been so much calmer lately since we hit the trade winds about three days ago. Mom has been cooking super meals, and I can tell Dad is more relaxed. The wind is now behind us, so *Kluane* doesn't crash around like before. If all goes well, we will be in Hawaii in one more week. Fantastic! Hawaii, here we come!

CRUISING LOG BOOK

Date:	Time:	Course:	Speed:	Distance:	Wind Speed: / Direction	Barometer
30/6/87	0645 to 08 45	187°T	6½ Knots	13 N.Miles	17 Knots Easterlies	1010

Notes: Nice beam reach, easy sailing. Saw excellent sunrise today. Tropic birds are all over here — must mean good fishing! :) Sam

Satellite Navigator Fixes: 0 715, 0 750
Estimated Position: 15°N 155°W

June 12
Dear Diary,
   We're nearly there! I can't believe it. Ever since our three-quarter-way party, I haven't been able to think of anything else but Hawaii . . . icy cold Coke, ice cream, and a crisp red apple. Charlie keeps asking about going to the park—I think he needs to get rid of his energy. Mom is dreaming of soaking in a real bathtub, and I know all Dad wants is a good night's sleep.
   The temperature is really warm now. Yesterday, Mom packed away all our winter clothes into storage. It's strange that only last week we were complaining of the cold, and now I hate to admit that it's almost too hot.
   I hope we get there soon—these last three days are killing me!

June 14

Dear Diary,

I know we must be getting close because today I heard Radio Hawaii on my Walkman. Dad estimates that we should see land early tomorrow morning. I have nothing else to say but, I CAN'T WAIT!!!

June 15

Dear Diary,

Dad just radioed Hawaii Customs so we can be cleared into the country. He explained our position and expected time of arrival. We can't set foot on American soil until we have been cleared through customs, so I hope they hurry. After exactly three weeks at sea, I'm not sure if I'll even be able to walk properly on land again.

I think the arrival party is going to be the best party of all!

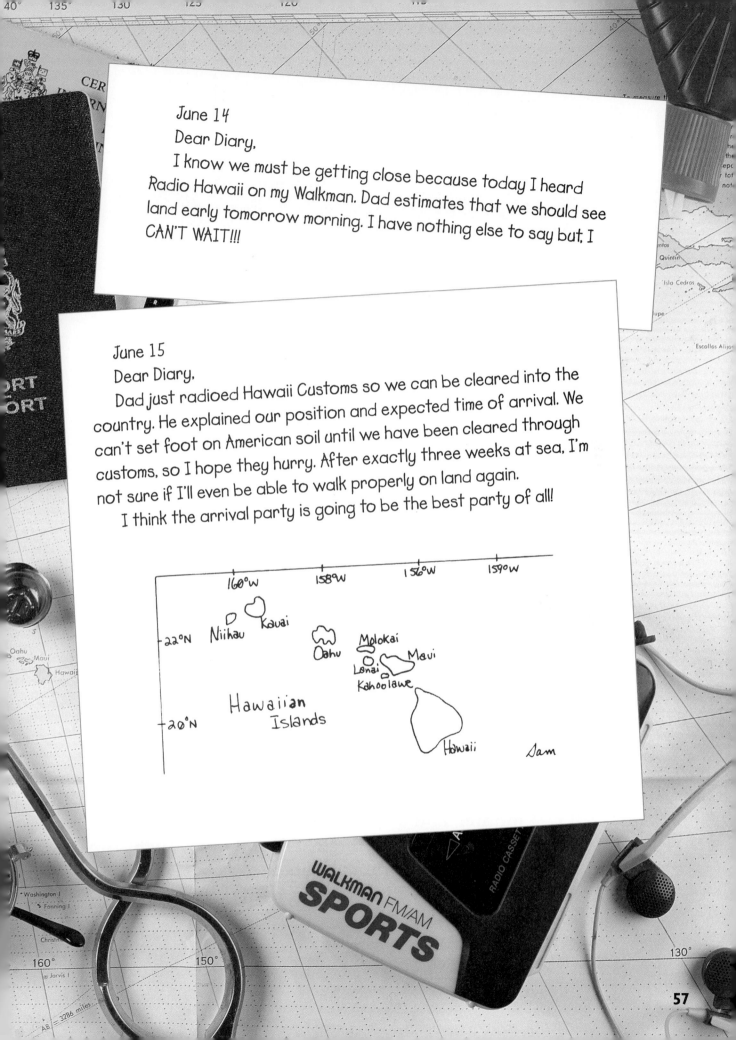

160°W   158°W   156°W   159°W

22°N Niihau Kauai

Oahu

Molokai

Lanai Maui

Kahoolawe

Hawaiian
Islands

20°N

Hawaii

Sam

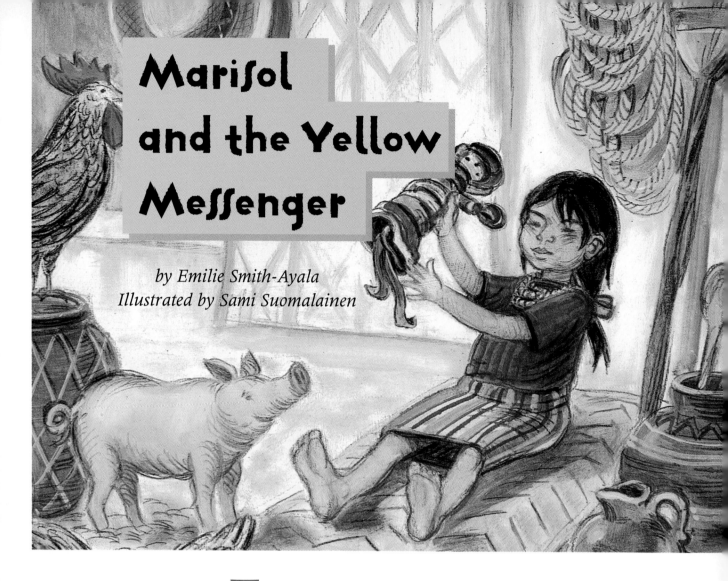

Marisol and the Yellow Messenger

by Emilie Smith-Ayala
Illustrated by Sami Suomalainen

This is the story of a girl called Marisol. In Spanish, Marisol means ocean and sun. Her parents gave her this name because when she was born she was happy and warm like the morning sun, and her eyes and hair were black like the deep ocean on a moonless night.

But a day came when her eyes changed and told their own sad story. When Marisol was only eight years old her father was killed, and she, her mother, and her little brothers had to run away to Canada. Every single day and every night the only thing she thought about was her beautiful country and all the things her father had taught her before he died.

Now they were in a strange country, where people spoke a different language. They lived on the first floor of a two-storey house on a busy street, with a laundromat on one side of them, and a grocery store on the other. Marisol didn't go out much. She played with her brothers, but they were small. Sometimes she tried to help her mother.

One day Marisol was coming home from school. It was getting dark even though it was only afternoon, and her breath made thin clouds in front of her face. She shivered as the icy snow drifted down, and she shuffled her cold feet. The snow was dirty from the cars and trucks that rumbled past.

She sighed and imagined herself back in her grandparents' house—she was rocking with her grandpa in the hammock after school, listening to the rhythm of the slap, slap of her grandma making tortillas.

She shook off the daydream when she reached her house. The family ate supper and watched some TV, but after awhile, tired of listening to English, they went to bed.

That night there came a great storm. The wind moaned and the snow blew around in big gusts and blinding circles. Marisol was listening to the whistling of the storm.

She began to think again of her grandfather and grandmother; then she looked at the big picture of her father above her bed and cried for a while. Then she fell asleep.

When the whole house and the street outside were still, Marisol began to dream. She saw four old women kneeling on the ground. They were weaving, pulling the weft thread through the warp, their brown hands working quietly, quickly. The women were dressed in brilliant reds, greens, pinks, blues, and yellows. They were women from her homeland, and the cloth they were weaving had every color of the world in it. Marisol was in the middle of their circle and they spoke with her.

"You know us, Marisol," they said. "We are your great-grandmothers' mothers. We are in the trees and the stars, the jaguars and the corn. We see everything and are touched by everything. Now look inside—your tears are ours, because your father was our son. And when he died our voices sobbed along with yours. We come to bring you peace. See how your father is with us now, and with you always. His breath is the wind that lifts your hair. His eyes are the stars that are watching you. So look for him everywhere, and don't be afraid, pequeña."

As she lay in their circle Marisol felt safe and protected, and for the first time a deep pain in her body began to flow out. She looked from one face to another, and the cloth that the women were weaving grew wide. It grew bigger than themselves and Marisol was surrounded by a giant multi-colored circle.

Then she woke up.

It was dark outside. The storm had calmed, and she listened to the breathing of one brother, then the other, then to the gentle sighs of their mother in the small room they all shared. She couldn't quite remember the dream, but she felt warm in her bed. Soon she fell asleep again.

The next day, the whole big city was covered in snow—so much snow that cars stopped moving

and school was cancelled. People got busy digging, and happy children bundled up and went climbing in the mountains of snow. Marisol and her brothers went out. They played in the snow as though they had lived in the north all their lives. They made snowballs and went sledding with the other children.

Finally, as the sun was going down, they ran home tired, cold, and laughing.

On the way down the street, Marisol remembered the dream. She remembered the words of the old women: ". . . so look for him everywhere." She looked around at the stillness of the snow. She did not see her father's face anywhere in the frozen white. The children arrived breathless at the front stairs. The little boys went in, pulling off their boots and talking both at once to their mother. But Marisol didn't go straight in. She stood at the door, waiting.

At that moment she saw something coming that made her eyes open wide and her hair tingle. Out of the white came a little yellow bird. It came straight towards her, and when she opened the door wide it flew in. There was a great uproar in the tiny apartment as the bird fluttered around, stopping here and there, looking at the people with

its little head tilted. They put out some water in a
teacup without a handle, and some sesame seeds
in the lid of a sour-cream container. The bird
landed to take little sips and pecks.

As darkness filled the streets outside, the little
visitor calmed down.

"We must let it go again," said Marisol's
mother. "It's not fair to hold it prisoner." But
Marisol and her brothers pleaded with her to let
the creature stay.

"It would die for sure out on a night like this," they said. So the little yellow bird with the cheery black eyes stayed. It spent the night in the warm bathroom, on a perch made out of a wooden spoon.

Before Marisol went to sleep she checked up on the bird one last time. It had begun to trill, it felt so at home in the warm apartment. As she lay down she listened, and it seemed to her as though the bird were singing, in a voice she had heard so many times before, "Don't be afraid, my little one, don't be afraid, my little one."

Marisol pulled her covers tightly around her. She smiled softly in recognition, and she felt a love for her mother and her little brothers that was stronger than ever before.

She knew why the yellow bird had come.

ABOUT THE AUTHOR   EMILIE SMITH-AYALA

Emilie Smith-Ayala was born in Argentina. However, she spent the first part of her life living in the United States and Canada. In 1984 she married a Guatemalan teacher. She published *Marisol and the Yellow Messenger* in 1994. Emilie now lives in British Columbia, where she is a storyteller, speaker, and writer.

My Wish for Tomorrow

Written and Illustrated by
Children Around the World

— Ow Chiann Huey, 8, Singapore

I would like to educate the people to share the world with animals and trees so they will not kill them. Everybody has its place: the animals, the trees, and us.
— *Kristel Acevedo Nevermann, 6, Costa Rica*

If a wall falls down cranes can build
it up again; but if a friendship wall falls,
it's you that has to do the building.
Stop fighting and be friends.
— *Meadhbh Long, 9, Ireland*

— Constanza del Pilar Morales
Gallardo, 9, Chile

I wish all adults would have a good heart that they will always understand the children.
— *Cynthia Barreda Vilchez, 9, Peru*

Wish: That young people wouldn't forget old people.
— *Renato Reyes, 4, Peru*

— *Samantha Louise Eddie, 11, Australia*

PEACE IN THE WORLD
All I want is a little peace please.
All I want is peace.
War in the world is everywhere.
All I want is peace.
I want peace in the North,
Peace in the South,
Peace in the East and West.
All I want is peace.
Peace in the hearts of all the leaders
in different nations of the world.
Peace is so great.
Thank you Peace.
— *Nadezsha Elizabeth Ann Perreira, 10, Guyana*

— *Samantha Louise Eddie, 11, Australia*

I wish everyone would love each other for what they are and that nobody would have to put on an act to be liked.

— *Akanksha Hazari, 11$\frac{1}{2}$, China*

We wish everyone could be kind to other people. We believe if one is kind to others, wars might be disappeared in the world.

— *Songyee Lee and Aram Lee (twins), 11, South Korea*

My wish is to make a big flying carpet so that I can fly on it around the world to make friends.

— *Sonali Handalage, 8, Sri Lanka*

— *Nery Briones Padilla, 11, Brazil*

— *Cheryl Loh Wai May, 10, Malaysia*

I wish everyone would be friends—nobody was ever sad and nobody ever felt left out in games and in the spring and summer months many fields were filled with sweet smelling flowers and the world was alright and safe. That's how I wish the world to be.

— *Rachel Tsang, 9, China*

— *Laura Capello, 9, Italy*

**If I was granted one wish to make the world a better place,
I would wish that people should live without fear.**
— *Danwathie Devi Persaud, 11, Guyana*

—*Tasha Jakimoff, 11, Australia*

I would like all cities to be designed
for disabled people.
— *Agnieszka Fiedler, 12, Poland*

**Wish: UN must make more
space agencies to know the
universe better (it is necessary
if we abandon this one).**
— *S. Özüm Basta, 11, Turkey*

— Jeremy Xie Wenqian, 8, Singapore

Peace is the best of my wishes. I would adore to see one day, everyone (all over the world) give a hug and say, How are you?
— Catia Sofia Feiléiro Lopes, 9, Portugal

A clean world.
A world with peace.
A fun world.
A better world.
A big world.
That everyone can be free.
That all this shall become true.
— Eduardo Blanco, 11, Argentina

— Peta Cassidy, 12, Australia

— Kathryn Stewart, 6, Australia

To have peace and health and trees for oxygen.
— Vicky Theodorou, 7, Greece

My wish is house.
— Fortunate Miambo, 7, Zimbabwe

I wish people wouldn't sleep in the streets and everyone would have a house, no matter how small.
— *Gyve Safavi, 10, Iran*

My wish is to see more happy children around me with more food and water on their tables.
— *Noura Basim Haddad, 8, Jordan*

I wish the world becomes safer for everyone and people don't have to worry about keeping their doors unlocked or even letting their children walk to school by themselves.
— *Rebecca Ann Story, 12, Australia*

I wish the world would be happy forever after.
— *Dumolone Dube, 6, Zimbabwe*

— *Mayra Garra Galma, Ecuador*

Born in Somalia

I was born in Somalia. When I was small, there was a war. My mom said that we must move from Somalia. We then moved to Kenya.

In Kenya, there was very little food and we were starving, so we moved again to Sweden. In Sweden we started going to school and learning Swedish.

My father came to Canada first, and then we travelled here after him. We used to live in a building on a road called Victoria Park. I went to a school where I started learning the English language, so that when I came to the school where I am now, I already knew most of the English language. I am very happy that we immigrated to Canada, but sometimes I think about visiting my country again.

Abdullahi Ugas
Grade 3

Abdullahi Ugas

I wrote this story as a journal entry for my classroom. I enjoy reading and I like to make up stories of my own too.

Peace

Peace is loving. Peace is caring. Peace starts inside us. Peace is not having racism. Peace is not fighting. Peace is having fun. Peace is having a great time.

Sylvia Tang
Age 9